W9-AAU-649

Uranus

by J.P. Bloom

ABDO
PLANETS
Kids

abdopublishing.com

Published by Abdo Kids, a division of ABDO, PO Box 398166, Minneapolis, Minnesota 55439.

Printed in the United States of America, North Mankato, Minnesota.

102014

012015

 **THIS BOOK CONTAINS RECYCLED MATERIALS**

Photo Credits: NASA, Science Source, Thinkstock

Production Contributors: Teddy Borth, Jennie Forsberg, Grace Hansen

Design Contributors: Laura Rask, Dorothy Toth

Library of Congress Control Number: 2014943778

Cataloging-in-Publication Data

J.P. Bloom.

 Uranus / J.P. Bloom.

  p. cm. -- (Planets)

ISBN 978-1-62970-721-1 (lib. bdg.)

Includes index.

1. Uranus (Planet)--Juvenile literature. 2. Solar system--Juvenile literature. I. Title.

523.47--dc23

            2014943778

Table of Contents

Uranus

Uranus is a **planet**. Planets **orbit** stars. Planets in our solar system orbit the sun.

5

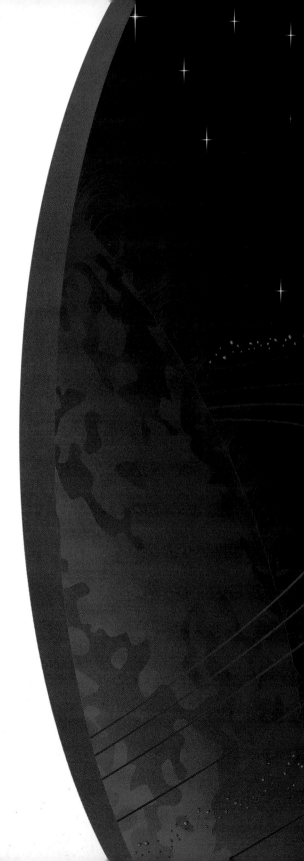

Uranus is the seventh **planet** from the sun.

Uranus is 1.8 billion miles (2.9 billion km) from the sun.

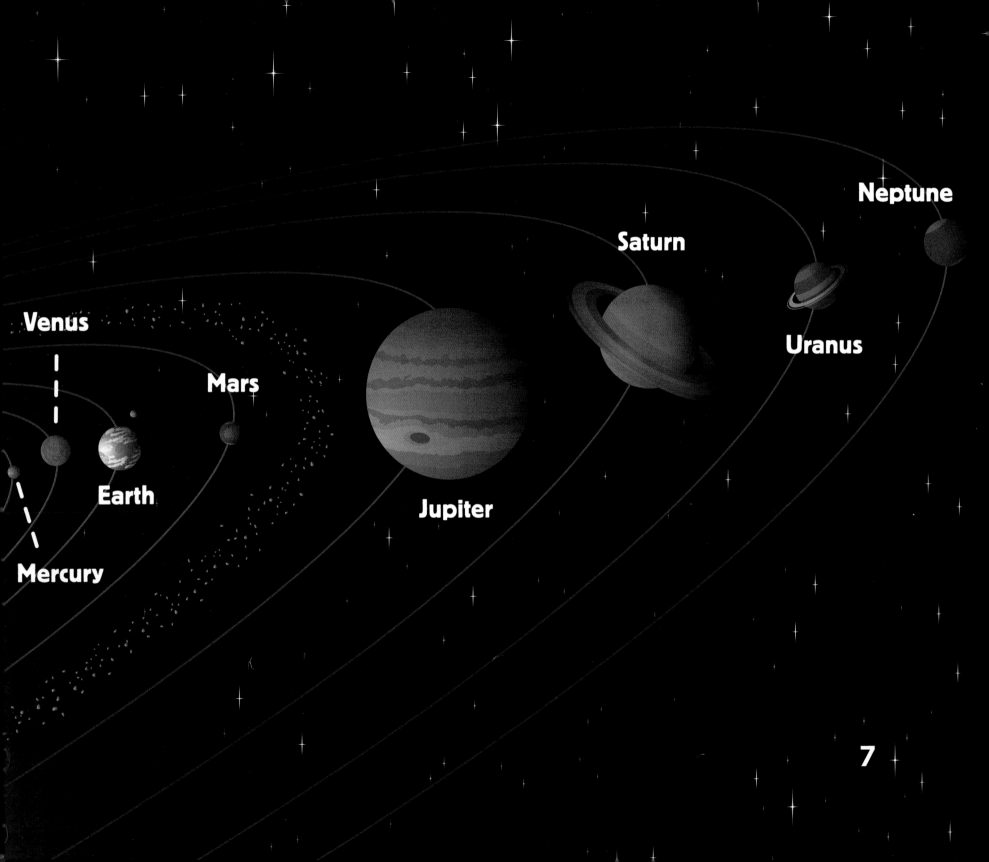

Venus

Mars

Earth

Mercury

Jupiter

Saturn

Uranus

Neptune

7

Uranus fully **orbits** the sun every 84 years. One year on Uranus is 84 years on Earth.

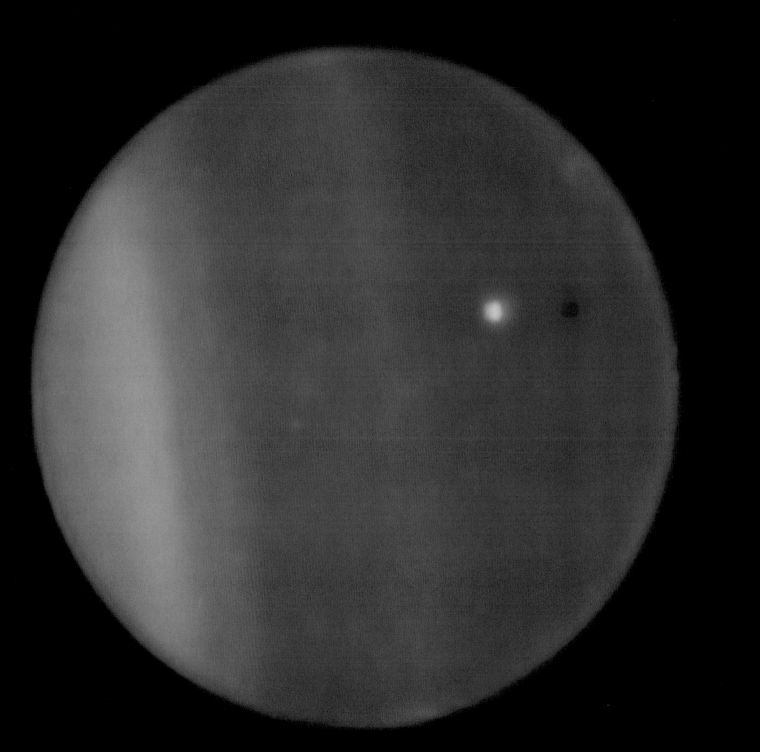

9

Uranus spins while in **orbit**.

One full spin takes about

17 hours. One day on

Uranus is 17 hours on Earth.

Uranus 31,518 miles (50,723 km)

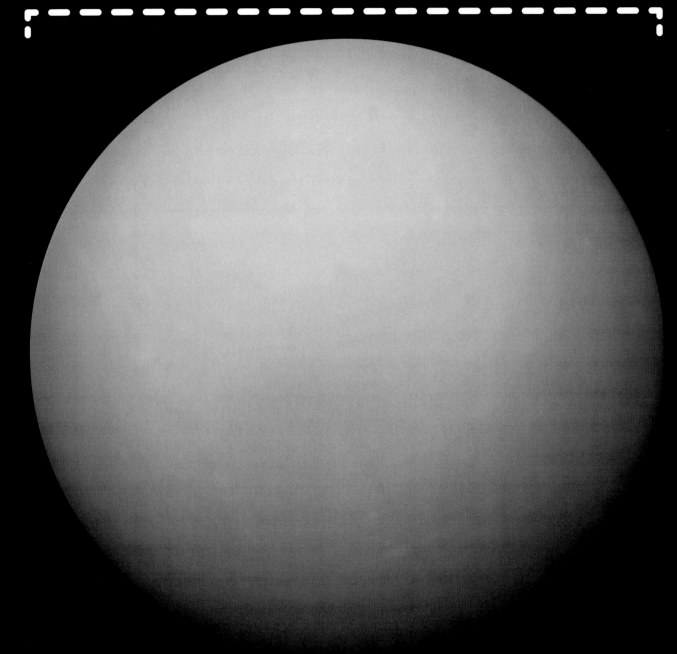

**Earth
7,918 miles
(12,743 km)**

Long Seasons

Uranus **orbits** the sun on its side. This makes the seasons last a long time.

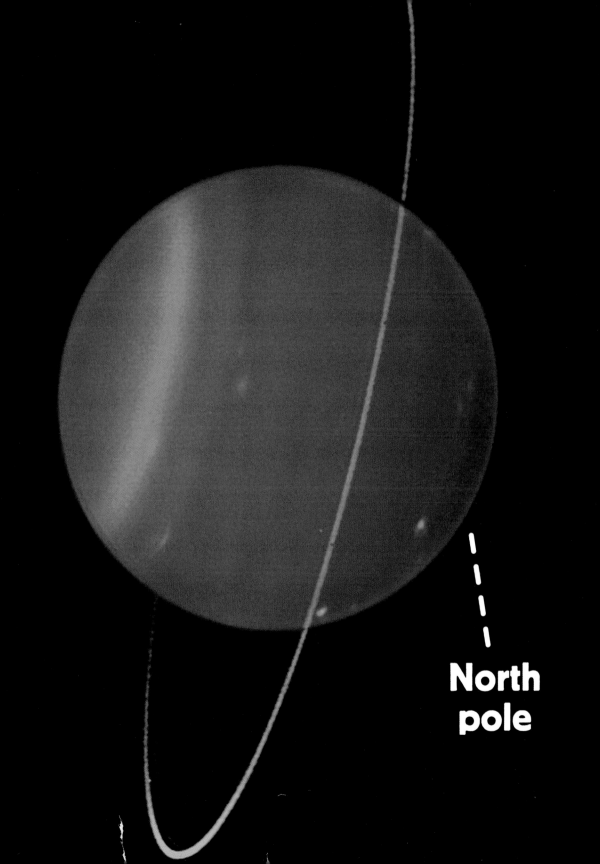

North
pole

13

For 42 years, half of

Uranus is in darkness.

The other side is in the sun.

15

Ice Giant

Uranus is an ice giant.
It is made mostly of
rocks and ices.

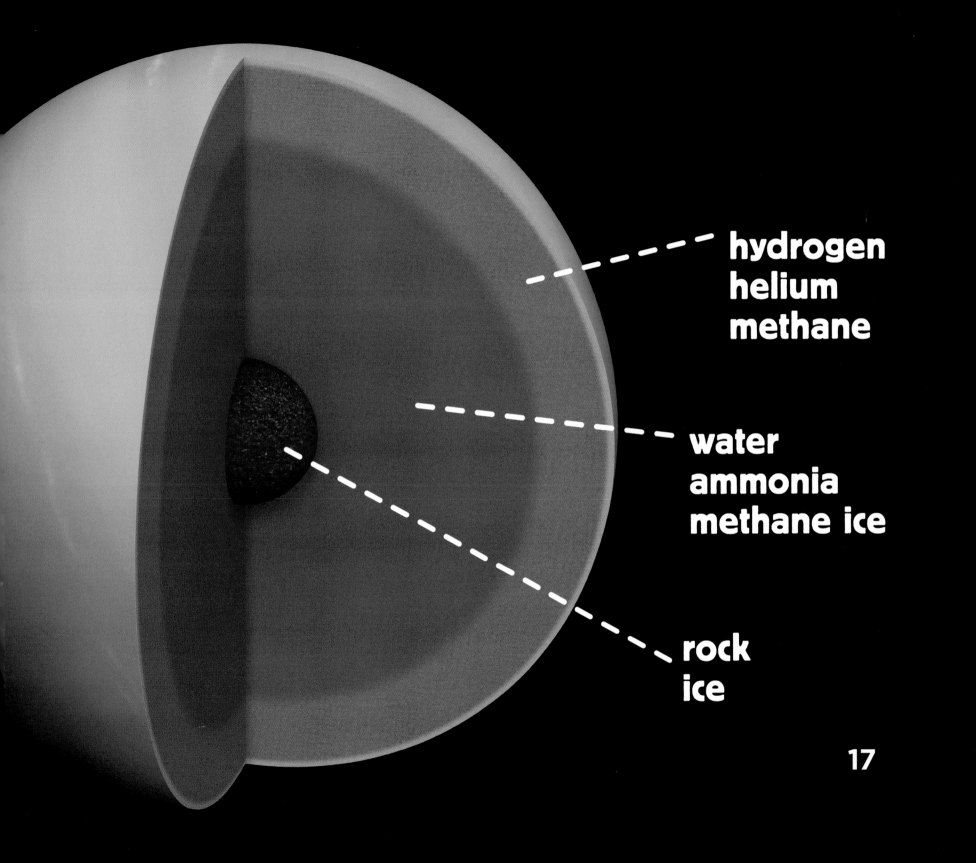

**hydrogen
helium
methane**

**water
ammonia
methane ice**

**rock
ice**

17

Rings

Uranus has rings. There are 13 known rings. Epsilon is the brightest ring.

Epsilon

Uranus from Earth

You can see Uranus from Earth on a very clear night. You will need **binoculars**. You will also need to know exactly where to look.

– – – Uranus

21

More Facts

- Only one spacecraft has visited Uranus. Voyager 2 flew by Uranus on January 24, 1986.

- Uranus has 27 named moons. Many are named after characters in William Shakespeare's plays. Juliet, Puck, Ophelia, and Stephano are just a few.

- A man named William Herschel discovered Uranus on March 13, 1781. Many people had seen Uranus before, but they thought it was a star.

Glossary

binoculars – a tool with a lens for each eye to see objects that are far away.

orbit – the path of a space object as it moves around another space object. To orbit is to follow its path.

planet – a large, round object in space (such as Earth) that travels around a star (such as the sun).

Index

abdokids.com

Use this code to log on to abdokids.com and access crafts, games, videos, and more!

Abdo Kids Code:
PUK7211